Depression

BY DEREK O'NEILL

You may order directly from www.derekoneill.com

For information about permission to reproduce excerpts from this book write to:

Derek O'Neill
244 5th Avenue, Suite D-264
New York, NY 10001

E-Mail: info@derekoneill.com

ISBN: 978-1-936470-29-7

First Edition

 It is not the intent of the author to offer advice in any form, whether it is spiritual, psychological, medical, or other. If you are in need of special assistance or advice, please consult with a proper professional. The information within this book is offered as an avenue to inspiration and awareness. This book does not claim to possess all the answers, nor to heal or counsel. If you choose to apply the principles within this book to your life, that is your constitutional right.

Get a Grip Series © 2012

Editor: Nancy Moss

Front Cover Design: © 2012 by Derek O'Neill and Clea Owens

DEDICATION

To all who read this book, I salute you for wanting to change the way you live for the better and for having the courage to be who you are as fully as possible.

To all who encourage me everyday to keep going and sharing their lives with me, family small and large. But most of all the little angel who came to teach me – Alexa, my granddaughter.

"Everybody hurts sometimes, and when we do it is nice to have Derek O'Neill around. His excellent little books on the things that get us, (fear, anger, depression, victimhood, mental blocks) allow us to find our way safely through our psychological minefields and arrive safely at the other side. Read them when you need them."

- Paul Perry, Author of the New York Times Bestseller Evidence of the Afterlife

Contents

Introduction

We've come a long way in talking about, understanding and addressing depression, and yet, there are still many misconceptions and hurdles that stand in the way of alleviating its appearance in our lives. My wish is to open the discussion here to include the way we define depression, the use of consciousness in finding your "true self" that exists independent of dark emotions, and how we can once and for all break free of negative programing that may have begun in childhood.

Depression manifests in many different forms and levels of degree. Help and support is an important element in diminishing hopeless feelings and charting the journey to happiness. It all begins with the decision that you're ready to change your life for the better. I am confident that you'll find some nuggets of wisdom here to set you on your way to transformative healing and joyful renewal…

Author's Preface

Thank you for purchasing *Depression - What's that?* This book has not come about as a result of my training as a therapist, but through some hard-learned lessons that I have experienced myself. This is how I know the path out of limiting beliefs and behaviors that hinder our growth. The tools that I offer in this book have worked not only for me, but also for hundreds, if not thousands, of people. I have shared these ideas in workshops, one-on-one sessions, and on my website. Through observation of myself and others, I have learned to identify the triggers and root causes of disharmony. Most of all, I have come to understand and utilize the best methods to achieve peace and balance again in life; not perfection, but real transformation and harmony that comes with learning who we are and what makes us tick. My 35 years of martial arts study has given me a refined sense of timing for when to strike with the sword to cut away old patterns and beliefs, and when to use the brush to paint the picture in my mind of the life we deserve and can have.

These 'Get a Grip' series of books offer tangible, authentic wisdom that will transform not only your life, but create a system for you that can help with all aspects of your life. You've made a great choice to invest in yourself by buying this book, or series of books. Let's change who we are together.

Derek

Depression
what's that?

What is Depression?

Whether you've experienced feeling "down" during brief periods in your life, or battled dark, persistent feelings of hopelessness over longer stretches of time, depression is something that so many of us have encountered. Often, a friend or family member is struggling with depression. Whether we are looking at depression within, or trying to help those around us, the place to start is with a clear, understandable view of just what depression is.

There are numerous studies dealing with the brain and psychology that look at the science of depression. Theories and therapies, old and new, are offered and touted as the way to relief and a more positive outlook on life. But what role does consciousness play? Is the inner sense of reality, the world within us that our mind creates, a key part of how depression manifests?

I'd like to share a little insight on depression. Depression is your way of saying "up yours" to the world! Though despair, pain, hurt and anger can be some of the catalysts behind depression, what we end up with is a reaction that has us withdrawing, not wanting to participate in life, feeling the game can't be won and we're throwing in the towel. No one seems to care about us, or so we come to believe, and we often turn that feeling of hopelessness outward. Depression can easily have us resenting, blaming, or disliking people. It can also leave us numb, unable to truly feel our emotions, and incapable to work through them.

Your mind, and what it is saying to you, is at the root of all your feelings. Depression is a stunning example of that. There are events and situations in our lives that bring sadness and pose huge challenges. How we treat these shifts is the difference between allowing ourselves to slip into depression, or realizing that we must change the way we think about emotions and feelings. When we stop avoiding, denying or wallowing in any particular state of mind, we'll be able to move through what may seem impossible to resolve.

It all begins with a sequence of very powerful words – "I am…" Anything in your life that you put the statement "I am" in front of will manifest much more easily than other perceptions and feelings. "I am depressed" is a statement that resonates. You begin to own those words, and become them. But is that who you are? Or does depression, like the ups and downs of life, and even illness (which depression is a form of) have an inherent nature of change and transformation? We may experience depression to varying degrees, but it is not who we are. Even if we feel stagnant, unable to see light at the end of the tunnel, healing is always there, and always fluid. You might want to begin by taking the word "depressed" out of your vocabulary, along with other negative words/phrases. Depression can last a long time when we "become" it and lose sight of its transient identity. Our mind is the only manifestation of our true and constant self.

There are times that depression can seem to take over our lives. We may also have family members or friends who are struggling with very dark feelings that can lead to serious consequences. It's important to get help when depression is severe and we, or our loved ones, cannot find a way out of despair. It is not your fault that you feel depressed. Sometimes no matter how much we try to shift our thinking, a mood of hopelessness can persist. Reach out and find a way to stabilize those feelings. Being able to gain control over your emotions and consciousness doesn't mean you have to go it alone when depression takes over. If you are experiencing this kind of deep depression, once you can begin to move forward, by way of outside help, the ideas and methods of transformation in these pages will aid you in continuing your journey toward a happy and meaningful life.

Awareness of the ability of your mind to change and grow is the first step. Consciousness is the most powerful tool in breaking the negative emotions that can cause a chain-reaction in our brains. Gaining the self-control over these feelings is often not easy, but if we begin to see the expansive nature of consciousness, as opposed to the "small mind" focus on our problems, the picture of our lives – the bigger definition – adjusts. How should we handle negative emotions? Is there a way to greet them with the respect they deserve, but then put them in a place where they don't spill over into our daily lives? How do you treat your feelings? Do you take care of them with kindness and understanding, or do you reject or fear them? Depression feeds on the resistance we have toward negative feelings. It's only when we see all of our emotions with a neutral eye that we can move beyond them and experience more joy and lightness than we might have thought possible.

What role does compassion and love have in depression? Is there a lack of self-esteem and confidence in evidence when we feel despair? Or is it an overly self-absorbed, egotistical view of our place in the world that leads to a focus of dissatisfaction with who we are and what life has delivered us? Are our expectations and desires making us unhappy? Where do gratitude, kindness and service to others come into play?

When you come to believe that you are a worthwhile, deserving person, whose happiness is not based on money, status or other external factors, depression loses its power over you. Though there will always be times of sadness where hope will be tested, no event or person can topple your consciousness of love and compassion. Are you ready to take an honest look at how your mind has been working and believe that dramatic change is possible? You have this potential within you, every day of your life. It's just a matter of owning that power, and not the depression!

Depression and the Self

Depression arises when we lose perspective about how our needs, both emotional and material, fit into the bigger picture of a happy life. When the focus is on "I," a self-centered view of everything that comes in and out of our lives is funneled through the ego. Though loving yourself and feeling deserving is at the heart of combating depression, so is letting go of the obsession with "self." This is a balance that may be tricky to achieve, but it's in that realization that we cannot control everything around us that we can overcome depressive feelings. This may be especially hard to see when you are mired down by depression. Often it's when people start to feel better that they can look back and see how they lost themselves by, ironically, narrowly focusing on their own assumptions about who they are, what life has to offer them, and most importantly, what they can give back to the world.

The difference in being upset or a little sad, and depression, is that we can sense the temporary nature of a bad mood or a small disappointment. Serious depression feeds on itself but if we can open the door to a better sense of "self," and see a bit of light shine through, hope and happiness will slowly but surely increase.

How do we form a positive, healthy opinion of "self" that can steer us away from an unhappy state of mind? Do you use the words "me, I, myself" all the time? Do you either feel wronged by life, or above it all, better than people and misunderstood by the world? Maybe you feel both extremes at the same time.

Where does the true "self" reside in you? If you want to begin to change the cause and effect of depression in your life, you have to look at the relationship you have with yourself. Depression keeps us from looking at this. It's avoidance, albeit often an unconscious one. The sadness and hollow feelings may be based on very real things, but going down the road of depression can be a distraction that obscures you from the direction you really need to look – inside yourself.

Do you feel like a victim of your past or your circumstances? Are you always comparing yourself, trying to figure out how to fit where you think you should be, or focused on impressing the people whose opinions you hold in high-regard? Where are you in this scenario? Can you find your true "self" - the person that exists on your own terms, and is not shaken by things in life that are beyond your control? When we are depressed we also lose sense of the past and the future. They merge into our present state of mind and we forget that things are always changing. None of us knows for sure what tomorrow will bring. When you make peace with that idea, a whole collection of burdens, including depression, is lifted off your shoulders.

When we keep saying, either out loud or in our heads, that "I am depressed," "life is awful," "I feel hopeless," "no one likes me," it begins to become a reality. How we talk to ourselves is a very powerful element in our sense of self-worth. If you keep confirming these things that you hold as true, they will manifest in the way you feel about yourself, and eventually in the manner in which people around you respond to you. Asking for help and connecting emotionally are part of being alive. But when you begin to believe your own negative words, and fill the energy between you and other people with these kind of declarations, there's no way to let the light in. When we become self-obsessed, we can no longer attend to our needs, nor our friends' and family's. Even if you can't see how happiness will visit you again, once the cycle of life changes, practicing some positive affirmation has a ripple effect.

Both negative and positive thoughts and actions are self-filling. In order to feel better about the powerful "self" that resides in all of us, you need to let go of the idea that you've been handed a raw deal, or that no one will ever understand you, or that the good luck that you perceive others as having has passed you by. Only you can make the decision to reject these patterns of thinking. Don't dismiss your feelings – face them, welcome them, offer them a cup of tea! But don't decide that they're necessarily the truth, based on some hard reality. They are only as real as your mind says. Feelings are fluid and life is continually changing, whether it seems that way, or not. When you are connected to your true "self," an anchor is created that can ride out the great swings of emotion with self-care and compassion.

Desire, Attachment, and Depression

Between birth and death we experience many desires. What are the first things a child needs? Love, nourishment and security. Does everyone get those needs met in a way that is strong, consistent, and uncomplicated? Do all children move into adulthood with a solid sense of wellbeing, self-awareness and compassion? Well, not quite. That's why therapists will always have work!

Love, nourishment and security are natural desires and essential pieces of the puzzle that make us who we are. More often than not, even a reasonably healthy adult will act out some form of unmet needs as an undercurrent to how they are living their lives. Problems arise and show up as neurosis. Neurosis may sound terribly serious, but behavior based on fear, insecurity, anger and a whole host of unresolved emotions, are common and widespread among us. So many of these feelings are behind desire. How does desire lead to depression? We think we need certain things to happen, for people to behave as we want them to, and to achieve material gain and outward success. Attachments to these expectations form, and desire becomes the basis for what we think will make us happy. Instead of looking within for happiness, we look to the outside world and external things, which fail to satisfy us in deep, lasting way. Depression is a natural result of this misguided disappointment.

When children don't get enough love, nourishment and security from their parents, say in the case of being raised by two alcoholics, there can be an underlying depression that carries into adulthood. Other situations and dynamics in our past may be very painful, and depression is a way to shut down. It's your mind saying, "I've had enough" and stomping off, wanting to quit the game and not participate any longer. Not getting your own way causes depression. When your desires aren't fulfilled you get depressed. Alcoholics are depressed – they're not living up to their own impossible-to-fill expectations and desires. They don't want to be here, so they slip into depression.

You cannot truly satisfy a desire. You may think you have, but it will only go away for a moment, and then be back. The only way to stop suffering is to look at the ultimate truth of everything: You are not permanent. You won't be here one hundred years from now. We get very attached to the present, along with our past, and what we want the future to bring. In fact, we become very attached to everything. The truth comes down to this - Either you're happy or you're not. The key to ward off depression that is based on low self-esteem and unmet expectation is to look at what you're attached to. It's not an easy thing to do, but you can take small steps towards that goal. Attachment is happening all around us. When dealing with depression, it can help to stop and ask yourself about the patterns of thought that you are attached to. Do you have a script playing in your head about the way you think of yourself? Are you creating scenarios about what you think you must have to be happy? Do you have firm ideas about how others perceive you, what you can and cannot do and how life is treating you? Think about not just the things and people you find yourself attached to, but what goes on in your mind. Can you begin to change your way of thinking? Is there a higher consciousness, which exists above attachment, that could free you from those limiting, preconceived ideas that have been formed in your psyche?

Everyone has a story to tell. We get very attached to that story, play it over and over in our mind, and believe it to be true. The story seems fixed, but, in reality, impermanence is the only truth. If you don't see that, you'll create more of those stories, and that's where the attachment takes hold. You may very well ask yourself, "Why does shit keep happening to me?" Well, because somewhere in your personality is an element that attracts that disharmony, and the experiences that come with that. Attachment to experiences – both good and bad – will always cause suffering and always cause confusion. If you understand that events are going to happen in your life and there is nothing you can do to stop them, you can begin to let go of attachment, and depression.

The physical world is based on cause and effect. Scientific studies reflect that fact. Any action that happens, results in a consequence. When an earthquake occurs in one location, it can upset the entire ecosystem. When you participate in an action there has to be a payback for it. That's just the way it is. We are seeing the results of greed on the planet right now, along with many more injustices being committed. But here's the thing – We need to stop blaming "them." We need to take responsibility for "cause and effect." We could have acted to change these things, even in a small way. We could have voted and spoken up. And if defeated, we needed to keep trying.

Similarly, you need to take responsibility in your personal and emotional life. No matter by who, when or where you feel you got a "raw deal," you need to detach from anger, resentment and despair. You may think you've already tried very hard to do that, with no measurable result. It's time to see how you are attached to those feelings. They may feel familiar and safe. The depression could be keeping you in your own cozy, albeit unhappy, little cocoon. If you want to come out, and experience a joyful life, you have to detach from that depression when you are ready to do so.

Getting help to gain perspective can be the start. Attachment and desire will cause suffering, and suffering will cause confusion. When you're in the middle of it you can't see the light through the haze. That's why you need to be able to talk to somebody. When you grasp onto things that you think your happiness is dependent on, it's hard to change your way of thinking. That's attachment.

Your Childhood Programing – How To Stop Seeking Approval and Take Back Your Power

At the beginning of our lives, we all start with a clean slate. Over time, as we move into adulthood, we become what could be called "walking computers" – programmed through our parents' relationship with us, and the events and situations that shaped us. From birth to the age of five every one of your bad habits, good habits, and values were installed in the new computer. Along with receiving – or not receiving – our basic needs of love, nourishment and security, we also learned about approval. Seeking other people's approval can be an element behind depression. More often than not, this begins at an early age. A young child experiences life very simply, but profoundly. When things are held back from them or, on the other side of the coin, when they are rewarded, it's approval, or the lack of it, that seems to determine that. The child will do anything to get that approval from their parents, but at a certain point, when it's just too difficult to receive, they may just shut down.

I have seen peoples' lives ruined because they tried to please their parents. Maybe they've trained to be a doctor yet never wanted to be one. The only motivation was thinking mom and dad would be proud of them. Then there are the people who hide their sexuality because they were terrified that their parents wouldn't love them anymore and now they see the world in those harsh terms. Soon, these people are living lies and losing the connection to who they truly are. The concept of unconditional love becomes impossible to grasp, and their whole lives revolve around pleasing others. This can happen in small ways, also, so subtle that we may not even be aware that we are pushing down or denying who we really are. How can you form a healthy sense of "self" if you are looking for approval from external forces? When we lose who we are, we become depressed.

The desire to be loved can be our worst enemy. That may seem like a strange concept, but love that is strong and constant exists without desire. We can want it, but unless it starts inside of us, we won't truly be able to give and receive it. Your hand has to be open to hold love. If you grip love, with attachment, it will become distorted and disappointing.

When you get to a certain age, and you are no longer a needy young baby, you have to stand on your own two feet. That begins with empowerment, and empowerment is about understanding and defining yourself on your own terms. If I asked each of you what you are getting from reading this book, I assure you I'd hear hundreds of different versions of what is being communicated. No one else on this planet knows the world that you live in as well as you do. And you will never know the world I live in or the person sitting to your left or right, because it's just not possible for you to see. Yet, you are your own unique individual, but you're also no larger or smaller than anyone else.

Sometimes depression arises because we think the way we feel, the things we want, and our life overall, is much more important, and dire, than it is. You are your own person who doesn't need approval from anyone else, but you are, also, just a single grain of sand on the longest white sandy beach on the planet. The beach is not complete without you but you are so insignificant in the bigger picture, that all you are is the grain of sand. When we live with an inflated ego as a centerpiece for how we feel and live, unhappiness follows. There's an easier, more joyful approach to living, which is all about letting the ego go.

Think about how you can empower yourself. It's not about becoming an arrogant, egotistical shithead who knows everything about nothing! We empower ourselves so that we can stop suffering. That requires each of us to set out on our own journey because there's nobody who can do that for you. If you're hungry, no one can eat for you! You won't feel very satisfied if they do, will you? There are people who can help you a to a point, but unless you're willing to take your own power and walk with your own intelligence and self-awareness, then suffering will follow you.

Stop giving your power away by putting people on pedestals that don't belong there. You are every bit as powerful as anyone else on this planet. When people whose approval you desire dictate your emotions – whether it's your boss, your family or your friends – depression sets in if you don't get the kind of feedback or result that you want. Are you waiting for a cue from someone else to make a decision? Do you blame a certain situation in your life for holding you back? What can you do to move forward, on your own, without approval from the external world? Life is a journey into the highest and most powerful part of yourself - your heart. When you feel depressed, think about the power you've given away. If you can reclaim it, you'll begin to see the way out of depression.

Mindfulness: Creating Consciousness, Neutralizing Our Thinking, and Learning From Life's Lessons

Is everything supposed to be perfect exactly as it is? Is there a divine accord that life follows on its own, in spite of you? Well, that would be absolutely true if we were in a state of equilibrium or balance, but we're not. We're either always running on a negative charge or a positive charge. We need to get to the level where we understand that we are creating our own reality. We're creating our own good fortune or misfortune and yes, depression. How do you change it?

Everything in your life is made from consciousness. When you can start to use consciousness in a more productive, positive way, you will be attracted to pleasure. There's nothing wrong with being attracted to pleasure, as long as you know that pleasure always comes with pain. Sooner or later, pleasure is going to fade. The goal is to neutralize these components of life. This is what yogis do. They have the ability to neutralize the whole game; that's why they can sit perfectly still. They're neither attracted to pleasure nor averted by pain. They just are. We should be trying to do the same, as best as we can. Set out to neutralize the way you see life, so that you aren't attracted to nor averted by anything. Just accept things for what they are and act in the moment. That's what "being present" in your life means.

Is it really possible to neutralize everything in our lives? Could you be just as unbiased about losing your house to the bank as winning the lottery? Well, that's the goal! What small steps can you take to get there? Maybe you can stop yourself from reacting with anger or fear when certain triggers are sparked? If you get into the habit of doing that, you'll avert unhappiness and depression. Denying your feelings or situation isn't the purpose of shifting your consciousness. It's defusing everything. It's saying "Hello feeling! I'm not going to react and respond to you in the way that I've been programmed. I'm going to go deeper, let you flow through my consciousness and neutralize you." Fear drives negative patterns of thought. Depression provides a veil to hide under. You're afraid you don't know how to have a good relationship, you're fearful you'll lose your job, you're terrified that you are never going to see change in your life. You may even be afraid to be happy, successful and feel good. How can your observations about yourself – the story you tell about you – be realistic when shrouded and painted by fear?

With so much emphasis on the physical world, the power of consciousness is overlooked. We often focus on the circumstances in our lives that aren't going well, instead of thinking about what is "right," that fuels depression. Over-emphasizing what we deem problematic is common, instead of looking at the bigger picture. When depression takes hold, our thinking becomes weighed down by negativity. Your mind is incredibly powerful, even in a depressed condition. That power creates more negative thoughts and more unhappiness. Depression is sustenance for more depression. Changing that "meal," even a little at first, changes consciousness. The results of shifting your consciousness are real and measurable. We are shaped by our thoughts.

What's your consciousness creating around you? Do you hang around with successful people, or unsuccessful people? If you're trying to achieve something, what type of company are you keeping in order to help that something along? What kind of company are you to yourself? You'll only get out of any experience what you put into it. It's not a coincidence who you bump into or that certain things happen. It is all showing you something. Even depression. If you want to stop doing something in your life that causes suffering and depression to yourself or to another, well then, you're going to first have to identify it. You're going to have to look at why you make those decisions or take those actions - either with help, or on your own. Only then can you make the change.

Life is continually offering us lessons. When you look at things that happen, perhaps over and over again, you may not know what caused them. That doesn't mean that you didn't create these things or circumstances. Somewhere in your past there was an event that matched the thing that is repeating itself in your life. Do you know someone who goes from one bad relationship to another? He or she tells you their new partner is different and then it all falls apart again. The person that they choose may be different, but it is the same lesson that your friend has to learn. That's how we humans are wired. Until we "get" the lesson that's being given to us, it continues to manifest. Breaking patterns that lead to unhappiness and depression takes so long because we fail to see the bigger picture of how our lessons are telling us something has to change. Even though we may acknowledge them in the moment, the little daily lessons build and build if not acted on. Then you have what was originally a small problem turning into a huge hurdle! And what happens is if you continue to ignore these little lessons? You'll feel frustrated, miserable, or even physically ill. Your mind and body will tell you your not taking care of yourself by learning from these lessons.

What patterns do you see in the choices you've made? Is there a certain comfort in keeping yourself from acting on life's lessons? Though change can be difficult to set into motion, just think of how great it will feel to finally learn from your past programming and rewire your life.

Gratitude and Service

We all need to look inward, but to do so with blinders on to the rest of the world, self-absorbed and thinking that your physical and mental state is more important than anyone else's, is what brings depression. Remembering what you are grateful for, and doing what you can to help other people, gives you a clear, truer picture of "what it's all about." Although consciousness, self-knowledge and responsibility for your own life are your goals, it's not all about you. It's not your fault if you are depressed, especially if it's become severe and hard to navigate, but shifting your ego from a place of all-importance to a bigger picture of the transient nature of life is a huge step in achieving inner-peace and happiness.

Depression places you below other people, yet above them, at the same time. You think you don't deserve anything, or that your desires will never be met, but overall, your problems are tantamount, and egocentric, in your mind. When you finally begin to love your self, desires begin to drop away. You need to acknowledge that you, like EVERYONE else, are a perfect miracle. Stop hiding your brilliance and understand that you are the greatest creation that ever was or ever will be, and then desires begin to drop away. If you think your life is awful, forgetting what you have – eyes that can see, clean water to drink, someone who cares about you (even if it's just one person!) – you can only see yourself. Are you reasonably healthy? Then you are very lucky, and I'm sure there are many other things and situations that make that true. We have forgotten to say "thank you." We focus on what is "wrong" instead of wonderfully right.

What about when we are faced with huge challenges, even life threatening?

There is still gratitude. When we lose that, there is suffering and depression. Fear, pain, unhappiness, all of it, are messengers that something is wrong. We can always figure out what lies behind our despair, and we should, but instead of shooting the messengers, try to listen to them and change your desires. When you desire less, happiness comes. Buy fewer things, reuse, travel lightly, and desire less. Be open to everything that's comes to you, without labeling them "good" or "bad," Your stress levels will lower and you'll be so happy, you'll be walking around with a fantastic grin on your face!

When people are depressed they can't see beyond their own world. Though there can certainly be external events and situations that are connected to depression, the mind often spirals out of control, focused on suffering and compounding the anguish. If you can reach out to help someone else, even in the smallest way, the whole dynamic of depressed, negative thinking can shift. It may be the last thing that someone who is depressed feels they are capable of, but it is often one of the most important components of healing. Service will always bring the correct perspective to self-centered, obsessive thoughts. The "self" is off-kilter when you are depressed. Service brings you into alignment.

The Depression That Lies Under Anger, Grief and Addiction

Anger may not look like depression, but they are different manifestations of the same thing. Anger is energy projected outwards and depression is energy projected inwards. It is the friction of you going in one direction and the impermanent nature of the world tugging you in another direction. With depression, you shutdown and suppress the issues that are bothering you. Maybe you learned that your feelings were not welcome in the house you grew up in and you pushed them away. You may be closing your heart, resisting love, because you were hurt in the past. You don't see the love that is inherent in the universe, no matter how much pain and suffering there is, and that starts inside each and every one of us.

You have to deal with anger and depression by surrendering and realizing that everything is a lesson. You are only here to experience life. The fact that you are not getting what you want can be simply healed by wanting what you get. Success is getting what you want; happiness is accepting and cherishing what you get. You many not have had the kind of parents you think you should have had; that they screwed you up in a way that keeps you from living a full and happy life. You turn the anger in on yourself and it turns into depression.

What you have to do is find the compassion in your own heart to love yourself, and even the parents or other people in your life, that you feel anger toward. Try to get over the fact that they aren't acting the way that you want them to. You don't control them. You are the one who has to take care of yourself. This shift – from anger to love, acceptance and self-preservation – is a big step in changing the pattern of depression.

When you have moments of frustration, you don't have to continue to walk further down that path. You can stop for a moment and say, "Hang on a moment. What's behind my feeling and how can I let it go?" You have to pause when you are in emotion and even physical pain. You do this stop by going within and experiencing your Divine nature of consciousness.

As much as depression can obscure the happiness that is available to you, knowing that things change – always – is important to remember. There are situations, circumstances, events and relationships that seem set in stone, but that are actually just as transient as anything else in this life. Do you have anger towards someone or something that feels like it will never subside? Are you grieving over the loss of a loved one and the pain seems insurmountable? If you deny that life is going to have these sources of suffering, depression can take hold. Life will deliver pain; there's just no way around it! What you do with that pain, how you see it in the bigger picture and your mindfulness about the impermanence of anything in this world, will guide you. Just like the goal of letting go of desire, attachment and expectation, you have to acknowledge depression, and then look beyond it. There is no schedule for how long that takes, and no wrong choice for how you choose to deal with depression, but working through anger, grief and disappointment, and letting them go, is key to jump-starting change in your life. Once you detach from thinking you can have life just the way you want it, you'll be much happier. That control you keep trying to grab is a heavy burden and a losing battle. It makes perfect sense that you would become depressed chasing what is impossible to have – power over anything but your mind.

What role does depression play in addiction? Some people would say that an addiction is a way of masking emotions or issues. Others would say it is giving your power to a substance, allowing something to take control of your life. Some others might say that people can't stand life, so they want to numb themselves or distract themselves, preferring to be high rather than deal with reality. A harsher way to describe addiction is to say that it is a coward's form of slow suicide.

All of these descriptions cover the basics of what an addiction is but we need to look at it through the lens of depression. Addiction is depression backwards. Depression is a decision by people, either consciously or unconsciously, to refuse to participate in life. Depression is anger without enthusiasm. The "backwards" part comes in when the enthusiasm is misplaced into drugs, sex, food, money, people, places, or things. Addiction is also an attachment to something. When you are attached to something, you believe that you can't live without it. That belief creates a fear of losing it and the need to control. The more you try to control it, the more deeply ingrained the attachment becomes.

In order to be free, we have to let go and change any and all addictions. It takes discipline, concentration, and effort. The easiest way to let go of an addiction is to have it 100%. Most people who have addictions try to balance their life with their addiction, and they manage to keep the addiction going for years. They don't want to have the addiction to take over; they only want to make themselves numb without suffering the consequences of the addiction. Sometimes reaching a "bottom," where life goes off the rails, is when we can finally see the truth of what an addiction is doing to us, and climb out of it.

When we do that labeling of "bad" and "good," especially when it comes to addictive behavior and habits, change becomes difficult. We need to neutralize the way we think of everything in life, even things that are destructive to people. If we are constantly judging ourselves, or others, we lose the ease to move from one situation to the next. Sobriety or stopping any other habit is a much better choice for us, and can even save our lives, but even on the other side of an addiction, there has to be sense of the pendulum swinging back and forth in life. We are not "good" or "bad," nor are our habits – they, and we, just "are."

Getting Help – Are We Overmedicating?

While in some cases medication for depression can be helpful, you have to understand its purpose. Doctors have pills for every ill. Many people need medication so that they can get to a place where they can see a way out of the depression and make a transition. The best way to approach being on medication is that you take it until you don't need it anymore. Yet some people take the medication and think they don't have to work on the underlying reasons that they are depressed. The medication is just covering what needs to come out, be confronted and let go of. With the use of medication so widespread, and overly prescribed, there are people who probably don't need pills ask to be put on them so they will have something in common with all the other pill-takers, and feel like they fit in. Again, this just masks and distracts us from the changes from within our minds that we need to address when dealing with depression.

With or without the use of medication, beginning to practice non-attachment and working against self-centeredness, are the true ways out of depression. If you can start to see how you are absorbed in your own mind, perhaps forgetting your connection to others and all that you can do not just for you, but also for them, transformation is possible. Small things - a kind word for someone, forcing yourself to go to the store for a few things, cleaning your desk, calling a family member to see how they are, etc. - all add up and begin to create positive energy. Just as is the case with negative energy, those actions and words feed on one another and grow. Positive energy reveals the world as it is – balanced and neutralized. You are responsible for your mind, but it's important to be kind to yourself and not place blame inward (or outward) on depression. We can't control it if we are unable to see out of the dark cave it sometimes feels like. Acceptance of whatever you are feeling is the way out of that cave. Seeking help, and being ready to take the first small steps toward self-love, compassion for others, and non-attachment, will begin the process.

What Can You Do To Combat Depression?

Discovering the underlying issues in your life that are causing depression takes commitment and time. What can you do right now, in partnership with the deep reflection it takes for long-term healing?

- Stay healthy by sleeping enough, exercise, keeping out of the sun, staying away from alcohol and drugs, and following a healthy diet.
- Challenge negative thoughts and thought patterns, identifying the feelings that add to your depression will help you to change your negative mindset. Why not start by making a list of the things you like about yourself, and the things that increase your self-esteem?

- Ask for help if you need it. There is no shame in needing support with depression. In some cases depression is caused by a physical problem rather than an emotional one, so have a chat with your doctor. If you have thoughts about self-harm or suicide, seek professional help, which can be very helpful.
- Build relationships, supportive relationships with friends and family, they're usually glad to be there, sometimes only to listen. Also, socialize even when you don't feel like it. If you make an effort to go out, you might find that the depression will be exchanged by more positive energy. You might have to "fake it until you make it." In other words, your mind sees what it achieves. To do this you need to pretend you're happy even when you're not. I know this might sound difficult but it is very helpful.

- Light a candle and sit with yourself for a while. Watch how your negative thoughts begin to affect your body and then immediately change those negative feelings to happy ones. Brighten them up with color. Put sunshine, trees and birds singing in the thoughts! This is very helpful for beginning to break down and change patterns.
- Proper breathing helps to balance and to produce calmness and happiness. If you are unhappy, perhaps you are not breathing properly. Improper breathing often influences fear, anger, depression, and negative emotions. Deep and regular breathing eliminates negative emotions and allows your brain to function so that you can contemplate and focus on what needs to be done. It also creates a space into which you can pour love and compassion.

- Bring a meditation practice into your life. Meditation brings calmness, relaxation, creating the right foundation for positive affirmations. Through meditation you can train your mind to steer away from the chain of negative thoughts and thinking.

Life is full of joy and fun when you just stop taking it so seriously. There is nothing worth worrying about. Nothing. Death is going to come to every one of us. Allow the Universe to just give you what it naturally wants to. Be open to everything, including life's miracles. The Universe wants to make you happy because you are happy. Your consciousness is pure as the driven snow. It's you that's tipped it either one way or the other because of your actions or your ignorance or your lack of knowledge or whatever you want to call it. If you want to be happier, start to put some sort of agenda in place. Make a conscious effort to smile more, which will shoot endorphins into your body! You've got to put an effort into it, even if you are depressed. Through help and self-awareness, get yourself to that place where you can see healing and transformation. Keep going until you are there!

ABOUT THE AUTHOR

For more than 15 years, Derek O'Neill has been transforming the lives of thousands of people around the world for the better. An internationally acclaimed transformational therapist, motivational speaker, author, martial arts sensei and humanitarian, Derek inspires and uplifts people from all walks of life through his workshops, consultations, speaking engagements, media, and tireless humanitarian work.

Drawing on thirty years of training in martial arts, which earned him the level of Master Black Belt, coupled with his extraordinary intuitive abilities and expertise as a psychotherapist, Derek has pioneered a new psychology, transformational therapy. His signature process, aptly named "The Sword and the Brush," helps clients to seamlessly transmute their struggles into positive outcomes, using the sword to cut away old patterns and the brush to help paint the picture of the new life that they require.

In addition to reaching large audiences through workshops and media, Derek advises individuals, celebrities, business leaders, athletes, artists, and politicians, helping them to find new perspectives on long-standing issues and bringing harmony back to their lives and businesses. Inspired by his worldly travels, he formed SQ Foundation, a not-for-profit organization focused on helping to solve global issues facing humanity today. In 2012, he was honored as Humanitarian of the Year and named International Celebrity Ambassador for Variety International the Children's Charity.

Author of *More Truth Will Set You Free* as well as the "Get a Grip" series and several children's books, Derek also hosted his own radio show, "The Way With Derek O'Neill," which enjoyed the most successful launch in VoiceAmerica's history, quickly garnering 100,000 listeners.

Derek is a master at offering practical wisdom and proven techniques for living a more harmonious and fulfilling life, bringing CEOs to the level of wise yogi and wise yogis to CEO; he has worked with executives from some of the world's major airlines, and the cast of *Spiderman on Broadway* to help transform group disharmony and untapped creative potential into productivity and dynamic performance. He has been featured in *Exceptional People Magazine, The Irish Independent,* and *The Irish Examiner.* Recordings of Derek's discourses are available for download, offering practical wisdom and proven techniques for living a more harmonious and fulfilling life.

To learn more about Derek O'Neill, to attend his next workshops, to order books, downloads, video streaming, or to contact him, please visit his website:

www.derekoneill.com

To discover more about Derek's SQ Foundation, the global charity that is changing the lives of hundreds of thousands of people around the world, go to:

www.sq-foundation.org

MORE RESOURCES FROM DEREK O'NEILL

Website: www.derekoneill.com

Audio downloads, Live Broadcasts, Books, Blog

"Get a Grip" Book Series

Happiness – You Must Be Effin' Joking!

Anger – Who Gives a Shite?

Relationships – Would You Want to Date You?

Depression – What's that?

Children's Books:

Water Drop Coloring Book

The Adventures of Lucinda in Love-Filled Fairyland

Social Media

YouTube

www.youtube.com/user/DerekONeill101

Facebook

www.facebook.com/derekoneill101

Twitter

www.twitter.com/DerekONeill101

LinkedIn

www.linkedin.com/in/derekoneill101